D0930383

MIGHTY MACHINES IN ACTION

Dump Trucks

by Emily Rose Oachs

BELLWETHER MEDIA • MINNEAPOLIS, MN

Note to Librarians, Teachers, and Parents:

Blastoff! Readers are carefully developed by literacy experts and combine standards-based content with developmentally appropriate text.

Level 1 provides the most support through repetition of high-frequency words, light text, predictable sentence patterns, and strong visual support.

Level 2 offers early readers a bit more challenge through varied simple sentences, increased text load, and less repetition of high-frequency words.

Level 3 advances early-fluent readers toward fluency through increased text and concept load, less reliance on visuals, longer sentences, and more literary language.

Level 4 builds reading stamina by providing more text per page, increased use of punctuation, greater variation in sentence patterns, and increasingly challenging vocabulary.

Level 5 encourages children to move from "learning to read" to "reading to learn" by providing even more text, varied writing styles, and less familiar topics.

Whichever book is right for your reader, Blastoff! Readers are the perfect books to build confidence and encourage a love of reading that will last a lifetime!

This edition first published in 2017 by Bellwether Media, Inc.

No part of this publication may be reproduced in whole or in part without written permission of the publisher. For information regarding permission, write to Bellwether Media, Inc., Attention: Permissions Department, 5357 Penn Avenue South, Minneapolis, MN 55419.

Library of Congress Cataloging-in-Publication Data

Names: Oachs, Emily Rose, author.
Title: Dump Trucks / by Emily Rose Oachs.
Description: Minneapolis, MN : Bellwether Media, Inc., 2017. | Series: Blastoff! Readers. Mighty Machines in Action | Audience: Ages 5-8. | Audience: K to grade 3. | Includes bibliographical references and index.
Identifiers: LCCN 2016033333 (print) | LCCN 2016035174 (ebook) | ISBN 9781626176034 (hardcover : alk. paper) | ISBN 9781681033334 (ebook)
Subjects: LCSH: Dump trucks–Juvenile literature.
Classification: LCC TL230.15 .O33 2017 (print) | LCC TL230.15 (ebook) | DDC 629.225–dc23
LC record available at https://lccn.loc.gov/2016033333

Editor: Christina Leighton   Designer: Steve Porter

Printed in the United States of America, North Mankato, MN.

Table of **Contents**

LOAD AND DUMP

A dump truck pulls up to an open **mine**. Its **dump box** is empty, but not for long!

dump box

Another machine scoops rocks
into the dump truck.

The dump truck drives to a **stockyard**. There, it tips the dump box up.

The rocks slide out. The truck dumped its load!

POWER MOVERS

Dump trucks are powerful machines. They move dirt, rocks, sand, and other heavy loads.

They are often used at mines and **construction sites**.

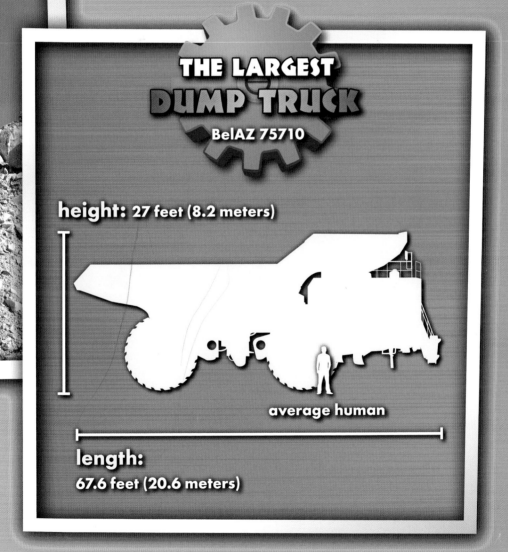

THE LARGEST
DUMP TRUCK
BelAZ 75710

height: 27 feet (8.2 meters)

average human

length:
67.6 feet (20.6 meters)

Most trucks empty out the back. Others tip to the side.

MACHINE PROFILE
VOLVO A40F DUMP TRUCK

length: 37 feet (11.3 meters)
height: 12.5 feet (3.8 meters)
load weight: 85,980 pounds (39,000 kilograms)

trailer

Sometimes dump trucks pull trailers to **haul** more on the road.

LEVERS AND HOISTS

Dump truck drivers sit in a **cab**. They use **levers** and knobs to control the machine.

lever

cab →

↑ ladder

Sometimes, drivers climb
ladders to reach the cabs.

The dump box is behind the cab. It holds the truck's loads.

hoist

To empty the truck, one or two **hoists** lift the dump box. Then the load spills out.

Many dump trucks have large, strong tires.

tracks

Others have **tracks** instead.
The tracks let them move
over snow or soft ground.

THUNDERING TRUCKS

Dump truck engines **rumble** loudly. The trucks beep when they back up.

Their loads can also **clang** and boom when emptied. This sounds like thunder!

IDENTIFY A
DUMP TRUCK

dump box

hoists

cab

big tires

Dump trucks drive slowly. They have to carry loads with care.

No matter their speed, dump trucks have important jobs!

Glossary

cab—the part of the dump truck where the driver sits

clang—to make a loud, ringing sound

construction sites—places where things are built

dump box—the container that holds a dump truck's load

haul—to carry

hoists—tools that lift and lower heavy loads

levers—handles used to control the dump truck's movement

mine—a pit or tunnel from which materials are collected

rumble—to make a low sound

stockyard—a place where rocks and other materials are taken

tracks—large belts that move in a loop around gears

To Learn More

AT THE LIBRARY

Clay, Kathryn. *Dump Trucks*. North Mankato, Minn.:
Capstone Press, 2017.

Meister, Cari. *Dump Truck Day*. Minneapolis, Minn.:
Stone Arch Books, 2010.

Smith, Sian. *Machines on a Construction Site*.
Chicago, Ill.: Heinemann Library, 2014.

ON THE WEB

Learning more about
dump trucks is as easy as 1, 2, 3.

1. Go to www.factsurfer.com.

2. Enter "dump trucks" into the search box.

3. Click the "Surf" button and you will see a
   list of related web sites.

With factsurfer.com, finding more
information is just a click away.

Index

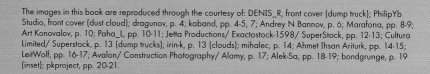
The images in this book are reproduced through the courtesy of: DENIS_R, front cover (dump truck); PhilipYb Studio, front cover (dust cloud); dragunov, p. 4; kaband, pp. 4-5, 7; Andrey N Bannov, p. 6; Marafona, pp. 8-9; Art Konovalov, p. 10; Paha_L, pp. 10-11; Jetta Productions/ Exactostock-1598/ SuperStock, pp. 12-13; Cultura Limited/ Superstock, p. 13 (dump trucks); irin-k, p. 13 (clouds); mihalec, p. 14; Ahmet Ihsan Ariturk, pp. 14-15; LeitWolf, pp. 16-17; Avalon/ Construction Photography/ Alamy, p. 17; Alek-Sa, pp. 18-19; bondgrunge, p. 19 (inset); pkproject, pp. 20-21.